IN FAIRYLAND

BY

RICHARD DOYLE

IN FAIRYLAND

A Series of Pictures from the ELF-WORLD

By RICHARD DOYLE

WITH A POEM
BY
WILLIAM ALLINGHAM
AND
THE PRINCESS NOBODY
A TALE OF FAIRYLAND
BY
ANDREW LANG

WITH AN INTRODUCTION BY
BRYAN HOLME

Biographical Notes by Dr PATRICIA THOMSON

A Studio Book
The Viking Press : New York

The Fairy Queen takes an airy drive in a light c

ve-in-hand, drawn by thoroughbred butterflies.

A *Webb&Bower* Book
Edited, designed and produced by
Webb & Bower (Publishers) Limited, Exeter, England

Designed by Malcolm Couch

IN FAIRYLAND first published 1870
THE PRINCESS NOBODY first published 1884

This combined edition with additional material by
Bryan Holme and Patricia Thomson
© Webb & Bower (Publishers) Limited 1979
All rights reserved.
Library of Congress Catalog Number: 79-4837
ISBN 0-670-39505-6

Published in 1979 by The Viking Press
625 Madison Avenue, New York, N.Y. 10022
Published simultaneously in Canada by
Penguin Books Canada Limited

Printed and bound in Italy by
Arnoldo Mondadori Editore

CONTENTS

INTRODUCTION

For many families, one of the happier trends in recent publishing has been the rediscovery of some of the wonderful illustrated books that date back to the Edwardian and Victorian periods. Among them, of course, were the handsome fairy-tale collections by Perrault, D'Aulnoy, the Grimms, and Hans Christian Andersen: those special editions with exquisite hand-tipped colour plates that our grandparents and great-grandparents loved to collect and that the children usually managed to coax one or another parent into reading to them at bedtime.

Belonging with such treasures, yet in a category quite its own – because never before or since has there been a book to equal it – is Richard Doyle's masterpiece *In Fairyland*, which was published by Longmans, Green and Co., in 1870.

Doyle's world of little people is a work of pure and utter enchantment. Royalty and pageantry rule the day, of course, for who could imagine Fairyland without a king or queen or a handsome prince and the fairest of all princesses? But abounding everywhere are the humbler souls, dozens and dozens of them: elves, goblins, kobolds and trolls, nymphs, sprites, and the most mischievous of all little creatures, the nixies and pixies.

The tiny people of this astonishing elf world are elegantly dressed and, for the most part, pleasure-bent, hobnobbing at dawn with the early birds, snail-racing, laughing and flirting prettily on stems of roses, feasting themselves to sleep on fuchsias, riding beetle-back to joust with each other at the tournaments, or taking airily to the skies with the fairy queen on a cabbage leaf drawn by spot-winged butterflies.

True artist that he was, Richard Doyle, or 'Dicky' as nearly everyone called him, believed that his watercolours spoke eloquently for themselves. He thought he might give a title to one of his little scenes, perhaps, or a caption at the very most to another – for the fun of it more than anything else.

The thankless task of creating a single continuous story around these highly individual scenes – the reverse of the customary procedure in book illustration – fell to William Allingham, a fashionable poet of his day who did the best he could under difficult circumstances. Among Allingham's more acid critics, however, were those who couldn't quite resist asking, 'Did he look at Dicky's pictures, or was he so carried away with his own rhyming that he quite forgot?' The lengthy poem didn't really make any difference to the sales of the book one way or another, because what the public bought *In Fairyland* for were the incredible pictures. It did make a difference, however, that these pictures had been superbly engraved and printed. This was due to Edmund Evans, who had the reputation of being the best man in the business.

In Fairyland sold out almost at once, and when the publishers ordered a second printing the result turned out to be even better than the first edition, a rare occurrence indeed.

Several years after *In Fairyland* had disappeared from the bookstores for the second and last time, a strange thing happened. The prolific writer and dean of fairy-tale editors, Andrew Lang, who had always looked with loving envy at Doyle's pictures and was confident that he could do much better by them than Allingham had, was permitted by Longmans to take the same engravings, cut them up, rearrange them, and trim parts off some altogether while he wrote an entirely new story around them.

The result, *The Princess Nobody*, published in 1884, was a smaller book which once again amounted to little except for the illustrations. But these, alas, had also suffered greatly at Andrew Lang's hands.

On the pages that follow, Allingham's poem and Lang's prose are printed side by side, for the dual purpose of completing this unique record and revealing the interesting comparison which these two entirely different interpretations of the same pictures provide. But the emphasis has correctly been placed on Doyle's inimitable work, all of which is reproduced intact here, as it was not in *The Princess Nobody*.

It is sad to think that for a whole century families have been denied the joy of these marvellous pictures. But, like the prince who kissed Sleeping Beauty awake after she had been lost to the world for a hundred years, and who was overjoyed to find her as young and enchanting as ever, we should surely be equally enchanted to find that Richard Doyle's *In Fairyland* has remained so too.

Bryan Holme, 1979

Triumphal March of the Elf-King This important personage, nearly related to the Goblin family, is
conspicuous for the length of his hair, which on state occasions it requires four pages to support.

Fairies in waiting strew flowers in his path, and in his train are many of the most distinguished Trolls, Kobolds, Nixies, Pixies, Wood-sprites, birds, butterflies, and other inhabitants of the kingdom.

A
FOREST IN FAIRYLAND.

DAWN.

First Fairy.

FAIRIES and Elves!
　Gone is the night,
Shadows grow thin,
　Branches are stirr'd;
Rouse up yourselves,
　Sing to the light,
Fairies, begin, –
　There goes a bird!

Second Fairy

For dreams are now fading,
Old thoughts in new morning;
Dull spectres and goblins
　To dungeon must fly.
The starry night changeth,
Its low stars are setting,
Its lofty stars dwindle
　And hide in the sky.

First Fairy.

Fairies, awake!
　Light on the hills!
Blossom and grass
　Tremble with dew;
Gambols the snake,
　Merry bird shrills,
Honey-bees pass,
　Morning is new.

Second Fairy.

Pure joy of the cloudlets,
All rippled in crimson!
Afar over world's edge
　The night-fear is roll'd;
O look how the Great One
Uplifts himself kingly;
At once the wide morning
　Is flooded with gold!

continued on page 16

THE PRINCESS NOBODY

CHAPTER I.

THE PRINCESS NOBODY.

ONCE upon a time, when Fairies were much more common than they are now, there lived a King and a Queen. Their country was close to Fairy Land, and very often the little Elves would cross over the border, and come into the King's fields and gardens. The girl-fairies would swing out of the bells of the fuschias, and loll on the leaves, and drink the little drops of dew that fell down the stems. Here you may see some Fairies making themselves merry at a picnic on a fuschia, and an ugly little Dwarf is climbing up the stalk.

Now the King and Queen of the country next to Fairy Land were very rich, and very fond of each other; but one thing made them unhappy. They had no child, neither boy nor girl, to sit on the Throne when they were dead and gone. Often the Queen said she wished she had a child, even if it were no bigger than her thumb; and she hoped the Fairies might hear her and help her. But they never took any notice. One day, when the King had been counting out his money all day (the day when the tributes were paid in), he grew very tired. He took off his crown, and went into his garden. Then he looked all round his kingdom, and said, "Ah! I would give it all for a BABY!"

No sooner had the King said this, than he heard a little squeaking voice near his foot: "You shall have a lovely Baby, if you will give me what I ask."

The King looked down, and there was the funniest little Dwarf that ever was seen. He had a high red cap like a flower. He had a big moustache, and a short beard that curled outwards. His cloak was red, like his cap, and his coat was green, and he rode on a green Frog. Many people would have been frightened, but the King was used to Fairies.

"You shall have a beautiful Baby, if you will give me what I ask," said the Dwarf again.

"I'll give you anything you like," said the King.

"Then promise to give me NIENTE," said the Dwarf.

"Certainly," said the King (who had not an idea what NIENTE meant). "How will you take it?"

continued on page 17

The Fairy Queen's Messenger.

Elf and Owls.

Saying "Bo!" to a Beetle.

Teasing a Butterfly.

First Fairy.
> Fairies, arouse!
>   Mix with your song
> Harplet and pipe,
>   Thrilling and clear.
> Swarm on the boughs!
>   Chant in a throng!
> Morning is ripe,
>   Waiting to hear.

Second Fairy.
> The merle and the skylark
> Will hush for our chorus,
> Quick wavelets of music,
>   Begin them anon!
> Good-luck comes to all things
> That hear us and hearken, —
> Our myriads of voices
>   Commingling in one.

General Chorus.
> Golden, golden
> Light unfolding,
> Busily, merrily, work and play,
>   In flowery meadows,
>   And forest-shadows,
> All the length of a summer day!
> All the length of a summer day!

> Sprightly, lightly,
> Sing we rightly!
> Moments brightly hurry away!
>   Fruit-tree blossoms,
>   And roses' bosoms, —
> Clear blue sky of a summer day!
> Dear blue sky of a summer day!

> Springlets, brooklets,
> Greeny nooklets,
> Hill and valley, and salt-sea spray!
>   Comrade rovers,
>   Fairy lovers, —
> All the length of a summer day!
> All the livelong summer day!

continued on page 20

"I will take *it*," said the Dwarf, "in my own way, on my own day."

With that he set spurs to his Frog, which cleared the garden path at one bound, and he was soon lost among the flowers.

Well, next day, a dreadful war broke out between the Ghosts and the Giants, and the King had to set forth and fight on the side of his friends the Giants.

A long, long time he was away; nearly a year. At last he came back to his own country, and he heard all the church bells ringing merrily. "What *can* be the matter?" said the King, and hurried to his Palace, where all the Courtiers rushed out and told him the Queen had got a BABY.

"Girl or a boy?" says the King.

"A Princess, your Majesty," says the Nurse, with a low curtsey, correcting him.

Well, you may fancy how glad the King was, though he would have *preferred* a boy.

"What have you called her?" he asked.

"Till your Majesty's return, we thought it better not to christen the Princess," said the Nurse, "so we have called her by the Italian name for *Nothing*: NIENTE; the Princess Niente, your Majesty."

When the King heard *that*, and remembered that he had promised to give NIENTE to the Dwarf, he hid his face in his hands and groaned. Nobody knew what he meant, or why he was sad, so he thought it best to keep it to himself. He went in and kissed the Queen, and comforted her, and looked at the BABY. Never was there a BABY so beautiful; she was like a Fairy's child, and so light, she could sit on a flower and not crush it. She had little wings on her back; and all the birds were fond of her. The peasants and common people (who said they "could not see why the *first* Royal baby should be called 'Ninety'") always spoke of her as the Princess Nobody. Only the Courtiers called her Niente. The Water Fairy was her Godmother, but (for a Fairy reason) they concealed her *real* name, and of course, she was not *christened* Niente. Next you may see her sitting teaching the little Birds to sing. They are all round her in a circle, each of them singing his very best. Great fun she and all her little companions had with the Birds; here they are, riding on them, and tumbling off when the Bird kicks.

continued on page 21

Musical Elf teaching the young birds to s

Rehearsal in Fairy Land.

FORENOON.

Two Fairies.

Greeting, brother!

    Greet thee well!
Hast thou any news to tell?
How goes the sunshine?

    Flowers of noon
All their eyes will open soon,
While ours are closing.   What hast done
Since the rising of the sun?

  Four wild snails I've taught their paces,
Pick'd the best one for the races.
Thou?

    Where luscious dewdrops lurk,
I with fifty went to work,
Catching delicious wine that wets
The warm blue heart of violets;
Last moon it was hawthorn-flower,
Next moon 'twill be virgin's bower,
Moon by moon, the varied rose, —
To seal in flasks for winter mirth,
When frost and darkness wrap the earth.
Which wine delights you, fay?

      All those;
But none is like the Wine of Rose.
    With Wine of Rose,
    In midst of snows
The sunny season flows and glows!

  Elf, thou lovest best, I think,
The time to sit in a cave and drink.

  Is't not well to have good reason,
Thus, for loving every season?
    Whiterose-wine
    Is pure and fine,
But Redrose-dew, dear tipple of mine!
    The red flow'rs bud
    In our summery blood,
And the nightingale sings in our brain, like a wood!

continued on page 26

The baby Princess is riding a Parrot, while one of her Maids of Honour teases an Owl. Never was there such a happy country; all Birds and Babies, playing together, singing, and as merry as the day was long.

Well, this joyful life went on till the Princess Niente was growing quite a big girl; she was nearly fourteen. Then, one day, came a tremendous knock at the Palace gates. Out rushed the Porter, and saw a little Dwarf, in a red cap, and a red cloak, riding a green Frog.

"Tell the King he is wanted," said the Dwarf.

The Porter carried this rude message, and the King went trembling to the door.

"I have come to claim your promise; you give me NIENTE," said the Dwarf, in his froggy voice.

Now the King had spoken long ago about his foolish promise, to the Queen of the Water Fairies, a very powerful person, and Godmother of his child.

"The Dwarf must be one of *my* people, if he rides a Frog," the Queen of the Water Fairies had said. "Just send him to *me*, if he is troublesome."

The King remembered this when he saw the Dwarf, so he put a bold face on it.

"That's you, is it?" said the King to the Dwarf. "Just you go to the Queen of the Water Fairies; she will have a word to say to you."

When the Dwarf heard that, it was *his* turn to tremble. He shook his little fist at the King; he half-drew his sword.

"I'll have NIENTE yet," he said, and he set spurs to his Frog, and bounded off to see the Queen of the Water Fairies.

It was night by the time the Dwarf reached the stream where the Queen lived, among the long flags and rushes and reeds of the river.

Here you see him by the river; how tired his Frog looks! He is talking to the Water Fairy. Well, he and the Water Fairy had a long talk, and the end of it was that the Fairy found only one way of saving the Princess. She flew to the King, and said, "I can only help you by making the Princess vanish clean away. I have a bird here on whose back she can fly away in safety. The Dwarf will not get her, but you will never see her again, unless a brave Prince can find her where she is hidden, and guarded by my Water Fairies."

Then the poor mother and father cried dreadfully, but they saw there was no hope. It was better that the Princess should vanish away, than that she should be married to a horrid rude Dwarf, who rode on a Frog. So they sent for the Princess, and kissed her, and embraced her, and wept over her, and (gradually she faded out of their very arms, and vanished clean away) then she flew away on the bird's back.

21

continued on page 27

Dressing the Baby-Elves.

A Messenger by Moonlight.

Rejected!

An Intruder.

Wood Elves at Play.

Flying away.

Some who came a-gathering dew,
Tasting, sipping, fresh and new,
Tumbled down, an idle crew,
And there among the grass they lie,
Under a toadstool; any fly
May nip their foolish noses!

             Soon
We shall hear the Call of Noon.

    They cannot stir to any tune.
No evening feast for them, be sure,
But far-off sentry on the moor.
Whence that sound of music? – hist!

    Klingoling, chief lutanist,
A hundred song-birds in a ring
Is teaching all this morn to sing
Together featously, to fill
The wedding-music, – loud and shrill,
Soft and sweet, and high and low,
Singled, mingled.   He doth know
The art to make a hundred heard
Like one great surprising bird.

    Here comes Rosling!   He'll report
All the doings of the court.

A Third Fairy.

        Greeting, brothers!

                Greet thee well!
Hast thou any news to tell?
Our dear Princess, what shadow lies
Drooping on her blissful eyes?
Her suitors plague her? – is it so?

    So in truth it is.   But, lo!
Who comes our way?   Fairy, whence?
Thou'rt a stranger.

Fourth Fairy.

              No offence,
I trust, altho' my cap is blue,
While yours are green as any leaf.
Courteous fays! no spy or thief
Is here, but one who longs to view
Your famous Forest; most of all
Your fair Princess, the praised in song
Wheresoever fairies throng.
Oft you see her?

continued on page 30

CHAPTER II.

IN MUSHROOM LAND.

NOW all the Kingdom next *Fairy* Land was miserable, and all the people were murmuring, and the King and Queen were nearly melted in tears. They thought of all ways to recover their dear daughter, and at last the Queen hit on a plan.

"My dear," she said to the King, "let us offer to give our daughter for a wife, to any Prince who will only find her and bring her home."

"Who will want to marry a girl he can't see?" said the King. "If they have not married pretty girls they *can* see, they won't care for poor Niente."

"Never mind; we can only try," said the Queen. So she sent out messengers into all the world, and sent the picture of the Princess everywhere, and proclaimed that the beautiful Princess Niente, and no less than three-quarters of the Kingdom would be given to the Prince that could find the Princess and bring her home. And there was to be a great tournament, or sham fight, at the Palace, to amuse all the Princes before they went on the search. So many Princes gathered together, all full of hope; and they rode against each other with spears and swords, and knocked each other about, and afterwards dined, and danced, and made merry. Some Fairy Knights, too, came over the border, and they fought with spears, riding Beetles and Grasshoppers, instead of horses. Next is a picture of a "joust," or tournament, between two sets of Fairy Knights. By all these warlike exercises, they increased their courage till they felt brave enough to fight all the Ghosts, and all the Giants, if only they could save the beautiful Princess.

Well, the tournaments were over, and off all the Princes went into Fairy Land. What funny sights they saw in Fairy Land! They saw a great Snail race, the Snails running so fast, that some of the Fairy jockeys fell off on the grass. They saw a Fairy boy dancing with a Squirrel, and they found all the birds, and all the beasts, quite friendly and kind, and able to talk like other people. This was the way in old times, but now no beasts talk, and no birds, except Parrots only.

Now among all this gallant army of Princes, one was ugly, and he looked old, and odd, and the rest laughed at him, and called him the Prince Comical. But he had a kind heart. One day, when he was out walking alone, and thinking what he could do to find the Princess, he saw three bad little boys teasing a big Daddy Long Legs. They had got hold of one of his legs, and were pulling at it with all their might. When the Prince Comical saw

continued on page 31

Cruel Elves.

The Elf-King asleep.

A Dancing Butterfly.

The Tournament.

Third Fairy.

Every day.

And is she lovely as they say?

Thou hast not seen her? Dost thou think
Blue and golden, white and pink,
Could paint the magic of her face?
All common beauty's highest place
Being under hers how far! — how far!

A glowworm to the evening-star.

Scarce Klingoling could say so well!
'Tis true: so much she doth excel.
Come, fairy, to our feast to-night,
Two hours from sunset; then you may
See the Forest-Realm's Delight.

But were it not presumptuous?

Nay,
Thou art, I ween, a gentle fay,
And sure of welcome.

It is said
Her Highness shortly means to wed?

Next full moon, by fairy law,
She must marry, no escape,
Were it marsh-sprite, kobold, shape
Creeping from earth-hole with horn and claw!

And hath she now a suitor?

Three;
Bloatling, Rudling, Loftling; she
Loathes them all impartially.
The first is ugly, fat, and rich,
Grandson of a miser-witch;
He sends her bossy peonies,
Fat as himself, to please her eyes,
And double-poppies, mock flow'rs made
In clumsy gold, for brag display'd;
Ten of the broadest-shoulder'd elves
To carry one must strain themselves.

First Fairy.

Aye! so I've seen them.

continued on page 36

this, he ran up and drove the bad boys away, and rubbed the limb of the Daddy Long Legs, till he gave up groaning and crying. Then the Daddy Long Legs sat up, and said in a weak voice, "You have been very kind to me; what can I do for *you*?"

"Oh, help me," said the Prince, "to find the Princess Niente! *You* fly everywhere; don't you know where she is?"

"*I* don't know," said the Daddy Long Legs, mournfully. "I have never flown so far. But I know that you are all in a very dangerous part of Fairy Land. And I will take you to an aged Black Beetle, who can give you the best advice."

So saying the Daddy Long Legs walked off with the Prince till they came to the Black Beetle.

"Can *you* tell this Prince," said the Daddy Long Legs, "where the Princess Niente is hidden?"

"I know it is in Mushroom Land," said the Beetle; "but he will want a guide."

"Will *you* be my guide?" asked the Prince.

"Yes," said the Beetle; "but what about your friends, the other Princes?"

"Oh, they must come too; it would not be fair to leave them behind," said the Prince Comical.

He was *the soul of honour*; and though the others laughed at him, he would not take advantage of his luck, and run away from them.

"Well, you *are* a true Knight," said the Black Beetle; "but before we go into the depths of Mushroom Land, just you come here with me."

Then the Black Beetle pointed out to the Prince a great smooth round red thing, a long way off.

"That is the first Mushroom in Mushroom Land," said the Beetle. "Now come with me, and you shall see, what you shall see."

So the Prince followed the Beetle, till they came to the Mushroom.

"Climb up and look over," said the Beetle.

So the Prince climbed up, and looked over. There he saw a crowned King, sound asleep.

Here is the Prince Comical (you see he is not very handsome!); and here is the King so sound asleep.

"Try to waken him," said the Beetle; "just try."

So the Prince tried to waken the King, but it was of no use.

     continued on page 37

An Elfin Dance by Night appears to be the subject of this picture at first sigh[t]
but a Fairy Queen may be seen seated in the foreground, and it looks as if she
and the Fairy King, who has gone up upon the toadstool, and turned his back[...]

pon her, have had "words." But it is supposed that the little creature
hispering in her ear brings a message of reconciliation; and that is why the
lves, an amiable race, are showing their joy by dancing like mad.

Asleep in the moonlight. The dancing Elves have all gone to rest; the King and Que

re evidently friends again, and, let us hope, lived happily ever afterwards.

Second Fairy.

This is more
Than I ever heard before.

Third Fairy.

Field-marshal Rudling, soldier fay,
His beard a broom to sweep away
Opposition, with his frown
Biddeth common fairies "Down!
"Down on your knees!" and then his smile,
Our sweet Princess's heart to wile –
Soft as a rat-trap! and his voice –
Angry jay makes no such noise
When bold marauders threat (as you,
Little Jinkling, sometimes do)
Her freckled eggs.

Fourth Fairy.

And Loftling?

True.
Prince Loftling's chin, so grand is he,
Is where another's nose would be;
His high backbone the wrong way bends
With nobleness.   He condescends
To come in state to our poor wood;
And then 'tis always understood
We silence every prattling bird,
Nor must one grasshopper be heard;
Which tasks our people; sweet Princess
Being nigh half-dead with weariness
Of ceremonial and precision, –
"Madam, with your august permission,
"I have the honour to remark –
"Ah hum! ah haw!" from dawn to dark.

He will not win her?

No, no, no!
Dreary the wood if that were so,
Good stranger.   But enough, I ween,
Of gossip now.

continued on page 40

"Now, take warning by *that*," said the Black Beetle, "and never go to sleep under a Mushroom in Mushroom country. You will never wake, if you do, till the Princess Niente is found again."

Well, the Prince Comical said he would remember that, and he and the Beetle went off and found the other Princes. They were disposed to laugh at being led by a Black Beetle; but one of them, who was very learned, reminded them that armies had been led before by Woodpeckers, and Wolves, and Humming Birds.

So they all moved on, and at night they were very tired.

Now there were no houses, and not many trees, in Mushroom Land, and when night came all the Princes wanted to lie down under a very big Mushroom.

It was in vain that the Black Beetle and Prince Comical warned them to beware.

As they marched through Mushroom Land the twilight came upon them, and the Elves began to come out for their dance, for Elves only dance at dusk, and they could not help joining them, which was very imprudent, as they had plenty to do the next day, and it would have been wiser if they had gone to sleep.

The Elves went on with their play till midnight, and exactly at midnight the Elves stopped their play, and undressed, and got up into the boughs of a big tree and went to sleep. You may wonder how the Elves know when it is midnight, as there are no clocks in Mushroom Land, of course. But they cannot really help knowing, as it is exactly at twelve that the Mushrooms begin to grow, and the little Mushrooms come up.

Now the Elves covered every branch of the tree, and the Princes did not know where to lie down. At last they decided to lie down under a very big Mushroom.

"Nonsense," they said. " *You* may sleep out in the open air, if you like; we mean to make ourselves comfortable here."

So they all lay down under the shelter of the Mushroom, and Prince Comical slept in the open air. In the morning he wakened, feeling very well and hungry and off he set to call his friends. But he might as well have called the Mushroom itself. There they all lay under its shade; and though some of them had their eyes open, not one of them could move. The Prince shook them, dragged them, shouted at them, and pulled their hair. But the more he shouted and dragged, the louder they snored; and the worst of it was, that he could not pull them out of the shadow of the Magic Mushroom. So there he had to leave them, sound asleep.

The Prince thought the Elves could help him perhaps, so he went and asked them how to waken his friends. They were all awake, and their Fairies

37   *continued on page 41*

Flirting.

Stealing.

Climbing.

Reposing.

> Kind Cap o' Green,
> I thank thee for thy courtesies!
> Brightkin's my name, my country lies
> Round that blue peak your scout espies
> From loftiest fir-tree on the skies
> Of sunset.   So I take my leave
> Till the drawing-on of eve.

> They call me Rosling, gentle fay.
> Adieu! forget not; here I'll stay
> To meet thee and to show the way.

All.

> Adieu! adieu! till close of day.

THE NOON-CALL.

Hear the call!	That fly or creep, –
Fays, be still!	Tree and bush,
Noon is deep	Air and ground!
On vale and hill.	Hear the call!
Stir no sound	Silence keep!
The Forest round!	One and all
Let all things hush	Hush, and sleep!

NEAR SUNSET.

Two Fairies : Rosling and Jinkling.

> Little Jinkling! friend of mine!
> Where dost lurk when fairies dine?
> All the banquet round and round
> Searching, thee I never found.
> Comest thou late?   The feast is done;
> Slowly sinks the mighty sun.

> Nay, fay!   I was far away.
> Over the tree-tops did I soar
> Twenty leagues and twenty more.
> Swift and high goes the dragon-fly,
>   And steady the death's-head moth,
> But the little bird with his beak awry
>   Is a better saddle than both!
> The lovely Lady of Elfin-Mere,
> I had a message for her ear.

continued on page 46

were dressing the Baby Elves. But they only said, "Oh! it's their fault for sleeping under a Mushroom. Anybody would know that is a stupid thing to do. Besides, we have no time to attend to them, as the sun will be up soon, and we must get these Babies dressed and be off before then."

"Why, where are you going to?" said the Prince.

"Ah! nobody knows where we go to in the day time," said the Elves. And nobody does.

"Well, what am I to do now?" said the Prince to the Black Beetle.

"*I* don't know where the Princess is," said the Beetle; "but the Blue Bird is very wise, and *he* may know. Now your best plan will be to steal two of the Blue Bird's eggs, and not give them back till he tells you all he can."

So off they set for the Blue Bird's nest; and, to make a long story short, the Prince stole two of the eggs, and would not give them back, till the Bird promised to tell him all it knew. And the end of it was, that the Bird carried him to the Court of the Queen of Mushroom Land. She was sitting, in her Crown, on a Mushroom, and she looked very funny and mischievous.

The Prince took his hat off, kissed the Queen's hair and asked for the Princess.

"Oh, *she's* quite safe," said the Queen of Mushroom Land; "but what a funny boy you are. You are not *half* handsome enough for the Princess Niente."

The poor Prince blushed. "They call me Prince Comical," said he; "I know I'm not half good enough!"

"You are *good* enough for anything," said the Queen of Mushroom Land; "but you might be prettier."

Then she touched him with her wand, and he became as handsome a Prince as ever was seen, in a beautiful red silk doublet, slashed with white, and a long gold-coloured robe.

"*Now* you will do for my Princess Niente," said the Queen of Mushroom Land. "Blue Bird" (and she whispered in the Bird's ear), "take him away to the Princess Niente."

So they flew, and they flew, all day and all night, and next day they came to a green bower, all full of Fairies, and Butterflies, and funny little people. And there, with all her long yellow hair round her, there sat the Princess Niente. And the Prince Charming laid his Crown at her feet, and knelt on one knee, and asked the Princess to be his love and his lady. And she did not refuse him, so they were married in the Church of the Elves, and the Glowworm sent his torches, and all the bells of all the flowers made a message. And soon they were to travel home, to the King and the Queen.

　　　　　　　　　　　　　　　　　continued on page 47

HIS is the Prince who travelled from a far country that he might place his crown at the feet of that wayward Fairy, who is seen seated upon her throne, a toadstool. He also offers her his heart, and his hand; and besides, he begs her acceptance of priceless gifts, which are carried in caskets of gold by his numerous train of retainers (Elves of the highest rank and first families in Fairy-land). There are earrings, necklaces, and bracelets of the most beautiful precious stones, — coral not more red than her lips, turquoises almost as blue, and diamonds almost as bright, as her eyes : at least, the Fairy Prince said so.

Enter, an Elf in search of a Fairy.

HIS is a little Play, in
Three Acts.

Scene : a Toadstool.

Characters : a sentimental
Elf and a wayward
Fairy.

He finds her, and this is the consequence.

She runs away, and this is his condition.

Of state?

               Of state: of import great,
I must not even to thee relate.

And is she fair?

               Thrice-fair is she:
The pearly moon less delicately
Comes shining on, than when this Lady
From her water-palace shady
Floats across the lucent lake,
And all her starry lilies make
Obeisance; every water-sprite
Gazing after with delight
Only wishing he might dare
Just to touch her streaming hair.
Meanwhile, crowds of fairies glide
Over, under, the crystal tide,
Some on swimming-birds astride
Some with merry fishes at play,
Darting round her rippling way.

There was your banquet?

                  There indeed,
Among the lily and the reed.
Wavy music, as we feasted,
Floating round us while we floated,
Soothed our pleasure and increased it;
Mirth and jest more gaily glancing
Than the water-diamonds dancing
Down the lake where sunshine smote it.
Bright and gay! — might not stay! —
White the hand I kiss'd, O fay,
Leap'd on my bird, and sped away.
Hast any news to tell me?

               Much!
Never didst thou hear of such.
  A fight with spiders? — hornets? — perils
Teasing owls, or chasing squirrels?
Or some little elf, poor soul,
Lost in a winding rabbit-hole?
Are the royal trees in danger?

continued on page 50

CHAPTER III.

LOST AND FOUND.

NOW the Prince had found the Princess, and you might think that they had nothing to do but go home again. The father and mother of the Princess were wearying very much to hear about her. Every day they climbed to the bartizan of the Castle, and looked across the plain, hoping to see dust on the road, and some brave Prince riding back with their daughter. But she never came, and their hair grew grey with sorrow and time. The parents of the other Princes, too, who were all asleep under the Mushroom, were alarmed about their sons, and feared that they had all been taken prisoners, or perhaps eaten up by some Giant. But Princess Niente and Prince Charming were lingering in the enchanted land, too happy to leave the flowers, the brooks, and the Fairies.

The faithful Black Beetle often whispered to the Prince that it was time to turn homewards, but the Prince paid no more attention to his ally than if he had been an Ear-wig. So there, in the Valley Magical, the Prince and Princess might be wandering to this day but for a very sad accident. The night they were married, the Princess had said to the Prince, "Now you may call me Niente, or any pet name you like; but never call me by my own name."

"But I don't know it," said the Prince. "Do tell me what it is?"

"Never," said the Princess; "you must never seek to know it."

"Why not?" said the Prince.

"Something dreadful will happen," said the Princess, "if ever you find out my name, and call me by it."

And she looked quite as if she could be very angry.

Now ever after this, the Prince kept wondering what his wife's real name could be, till he made himself quite unhappy.

"Is it Margaret?" he would say, when he thought the Princess was off her guard; or, "is it Joan?" "Is it Dorothy?" "It can't be Sybil, can it?"

But she would never tell him.

Now, one morning, the Princess awoke very early, but she felt so happy that she could not sleep. She lay awake and listened to the Birds singing and then she watched a Fairy-boy teasing a Bird, which sang (so the boy said) out of tune, and another Fairy-baby riding on a Fly.

At last the Princess, who thought the Prince was sound asleep, began to croon softly a little song she had made about him and her. She had never

continued on page 51

Feasting and fun among the fuschias.

Poor little Birdie teased.

Courtship cut short.

Dost thou mind the Blue-cap Stranger,
Brightkin by his name, that we
Met ere noontide lullaby?

  Came he to your Feast?

                    My friend,
Ask no more questions, but attend!
To the Feast he came with me,
The chamberlain most courteously
Placing us nigh the upper end.
Her Highness bow'd and Brightkin gazed
On her face like one amazed,
While the Princess's tender eyes
Rested with a sweet surprise
Upon the stranger-fairy: round
Went cates and wines, and Klingoling
With five new birds began to sing.
Then came a page on errand bound
To ask the stranger's name and realm:
"Brightkin, of the Purple Helm,
"From the Blue Mountain, fairy knight,
"Flown thence to view the Forest, – might
"It please her Highness."   It did please.
So by-and-by we sat at ease
In shadowy bow'r, a favour'd ring,
Now talking, now with Klingoling
Join'd in a chanting melody;
And evermore there seem'd to be
'Twixt Brightkin and the dear Princess
A concord more than string with string
To form the lute's harmoniousness.
At last *he* took the lute and sung,
  With modest grace and skilfully,
For tipt with honey seem'd his tongue;
  At first a murmuring melody,
Like the far song of falling rills
Amid the foldings of the hills,
And ever nearer as it flew,
Shaping its figure, like a bird,
Till into Love's own form it grew
In every lovely note and word.
So sweet a song we never heard!
When, think what came?

                    I cannot think.

continued on page 54

told him about the song, partly because she was shy, and partly for another reason. So she crooned and hummed to herself,

Oh, hand in hand with Gwendoline,
While yet our locks are gold,
He'll fare among the forests green,
And through the gardens old;
And when, like leaves that lose their green,
Our gold has turned to grey,
Then, hand in hand with Gwendoline,
He'll fade and pass away!

"Oh, *Gwendoline* is your name, is it?" said the Prince, who had been wide awake, and listening to her song. And he began to laugh at having found out her secret, and tried to kiss her.

But the Princess turned very, very cold, and white like marble, so that the Prince began to shiver, and he sat down on a fallen Mushroom, and hid his face in his hands, and, in a moment, all his beautiful hair vanished, and his splendid clothes, and his gold train, and his Crown. He wore a red cap, and common clothes, and was Prince Comical once more. But the Princess arose, and she vanished swiftly away.

The poor Prince cried, and the Princess vanished away, and thus he was punished for being curious and prying. It is natural, you will say, that a man should like to call his wife by her name. But the Fairies would not allow it, and, what is more, there are still some nations who will not allow a woman to mention the name of her husband.

Well, here was a sad state of things! The Princess was lost as much as ever, and Prince Charming was changed back into Prince Comical.

Black Beetle sighed day and night, and mingled his tears with those of the Prince. But neither of them knew what to do. They wandered about the Valley Magical, and though it was just as pretty as ever, it seemed quite ugly and stupid to them. The worst of it was, that the Prince felt so foolish. After winning the greatest good fortune, and the dearest bride in the world, he had thrown everything away. He walked about crying, "Oh, Gwen – I mean oh, Niente! dear Niente! return to your own Prince Comical, and all will be forgiven!"

It is impossible to say what would have happened; and probably the Prince would have died of sorrow and hunger (for he ate nothing), if the Black Beetle had not one day met a Bat, which was the favourite charger of Puck. Now Puck, as all the world knows, is the Jester at

continued on page 55

Amongst the sports and pastimes of the Little People, there was, once upon a time, a great race of all the swiftest snails in Fairyland.

This is part of the Triumphal Progress represented on a previous page; but owing to the delay caused by the tricks and gambols of the Elves, and the practical jokes of some of the birds, they have been left behind by the rest of the Procession.

A trumpet-blast that made us wink!
A hailstorm upon basking flowers!
Quick, sharp! — we started to our feet,
All save her Highness, mild and sweet,
Who said, "See who invades our bowers."

Who was it, Rosling? quickly say!

The King of the Blue Mountains, fay,
Seeking audience, without delay.
Fierce and frowning his look at first,
Like that uncivil trumpet-burst;
But all his blackness alter'd soon,
Like clouds that melt upon the moon,
Before the gentle dignity
Of Her, Titania's child, whom we
Obey and love.

Blest may she be!
But wherefore came the haughty King?

Hear briefly an unusual thing.
His only son, the prince and heir,
Kept with too strict and jealous care
Within the mountain boundaries,
To-day o'erleaps them all, and flies,
No elf knows whither: flies to-day —
The Lord of Gnomes being on his way,
Bringing to that mountain court
His gem-clad heiress.   Here was sport!
Then couriers told the angry king
They saw the prince on gray-dove's wing
Threading our forest; and again,
That he had join'd our Lady's train.
— "Madam! is't so?"   "If this be so,
"Great sir, I nothing know."   When lo!
Brightkin outspringing kneels.   "My son!"
Exclaims the king — "Ho! seize and bind him!"
But swift her Highness — "Stay! let none
"Move hand or foot!   Great King, you find him
"Here in the Forest-Realm, my rule
"Whereof no fairy power may school,
"Saving imperial Oberon.

continued on page 58

the Court of Fairy Land. He can make Oberon and Titania – the King and Queen – laugh at the tricks he plays, and therefore they love him so much that there is nothing they would not do for him. So the Black Beetle began to talk about his master, the Prince, to the Bat Puck commonly rode; and the Bat, a good-natured creature, told the whole story to Puck. Now Puck was also in a good humour, so he jumped at once on his Bat's back, and rode off to consult the King and Queen of Fairy Land. Well, they were sorry for the Prince – he had only broken one little Fairy law after all – and they sent Puck back to tell him what he was to do. This was to find the Blue Bird again, and get the Blue Bird to guide him to the home of the Water Fairy, the Godmother of the Princess.

Long and far the Prince wandered, but at last he found the Blue Bird once more. And the Bird (very good-naturedly) promised to fly in front of him till he led him to the beautiful stream, where the Water Fairy held her court. So they reached it at last, and then the Blue Bird harnessed himself to the chariot of the Water Fairy, and the chariot was the white cup of a Water Lily. Then he pulled, and pulled at the chariot, till he brought her where the Prince was waiting.

At first, when she saw him, she was rather angry. "Why did you find out my God-daughter's name?" she said; and the Prince had no excuse to make. He only turned red, and sighed. This rather pleased the Water Fairy.

"Do you love the Princess very much?" said she.

"Oh, more than all the world," said the Prince.

"Then back you go to Mushroom Land, and you will find her in the old place. But perhaps she will not be pleased to forgive you at first."

The Prince thought he would chance *that*, but he did not say so. He only bowed very low, and thanked the Water Fairy. Then off he set, with the Blue Bird to guide him, in search of Mushroom Land. At long and at last he reached it, and glad he was to see the little sentinel on the border of the country.

All up and down Mushroom Land the Prince searched, and at last he saw his own Princess, and he rushed up, and knelt at her feet, and held out his hands to ask pardon for having disobeyed the Fairy law.

But she was still rather cross, and down she jumped and ran round the Mushroom, and he ran after her.

continued on page 59

ATER-LILIES and Water Fairies of the period. Is it a grand aquatic procession? or is it only a party of Water Fairies disporting themselves? or are they racing? One Fairy Water Nymph is drawn on in her Lily-boat with the aid of a Kingfisher; another, floating in a flower, is helped forward by a Duck; a third is assisted by a flying Goblin. A Frog carrying an Elf on his back seems about to jump into the stream, out of which a Fish pops his head, and appears to be making a remark.

"Free came he hither, free shall go.
"I nothing knew that this was so."
Then says the prince, "If you command,
"I leave you, Pride of Fairyland,
"Else never!"   Briefly now to tell,
As briefly all these things befell,
'Twas clear as new-born star they loved;
The Mountain-King their love approved;
And all were happy.

        Where are they,
The King and Prince, now?

         Flown away
On the sunset's latest ray.
To-morrow they will come again,
With a countless noble train;
And next full moon – the Wedding-Feast!

  O joy! the greatest and the least
Will join the revelry and bring
A marriage-gift of some fine thing.

  I know a present she will prize –
A team of spot-wing'd butterflies,
Right in flight, or else with ease
Winding through the tops of trees,
Or soaring in the summer sky.

  Well done, Jinkling! – now goodbye;
Sleepy as a field-mouse I,
When paws and snout coil'd he doth lie.

  Hark to Klingoling's lute-playing!
On the fir-tree-spire a-swaying
Gently to the crescent moon.

I cannot stay to hear the tune.

I linger in the drowsy light.

And so, goodnight!

       And so, goodnight!

continued on page 62

So he chased her for a minute or two, and at last she laughed, and popped up her head over the Mushroom, and pursed up her lips into a cherry. And he kissed her across the Mushroom, and knew he had won back his own dear Princess, and they felt even happier than if they had never been parted.

"Journeys end in lovers meeting," and so do Stories. The Prince has his Princess once again, and I can tell you they did not wait long, this time, in the Valley Magical. Off they went, straight home, and the Black Beetle guided them, flying in a bee-line. Just on the further border of Mushroom Land, they came to all the Princes fast asleep. But when the Princess drew near, they all wakened, and jumped up, and they slapped the fortunate Prince on the back, and wished him luck, and cried, "Hullo, Comical, old chap; we hardly knew you! Why, you've grown quite handsome!" And so he had; he was changed into Prince Charming again, but he was so happy he never noticed it, for he was not conceited. But the Princess noticed it, and she loved him all the better. Then they all made a procession, with the Black Beetle marching at the head; indeed, they called him "Black Rod" now, and he was quite a Courtier.

So with flags flying, and music playing, they returned to the home of the Princess. And the King and Queen met them at the park gates, and fell on the neck of the Prince and Princess, and kissed them, and laughed, and cried for joy, and kissed them again. You may be sure the old Nurse was out among the foremost, her face quite shining with pleasure, and using longer words than the noblest there. And she admired the Prince very much, and was delighted that "her girl," as she called the Princess, had got such a good husband. So here we leave them, and that country remained always happy, and so it has neither history nor geography. Therefore you won't find it on any map, nor can you read about it in any book but this book. Lastly, here is a picture of the Prince and the Princess at home, sitting on a beautiful Rose, as a Fairy's God-child can do if she pleases.

As to the Black Beetle, he was appointed to a place about the Court, but he never married, he had no children, and there are no *other* Black Beetles, consequently, in the country where the Prince and Princess became King and Queen.

An Evening Ride.

Fairy Child's Play.

A Serenade.

Manners and Customs of some of the natives of Fairyland.

AFTER SUNSET.

Klingoling and a Faint Chorus.

Moon soon sets now :
Elves cradled on the bough.
Day's fays drop asleep :
Dreams through the forest creep.

When broadens the moonlight, we frolic and jest ;
When darkles the forest, we sink into rest.

Shine, fine star above !
Love's come, happy love !
Haste, happy wedding-night,
Full moon, round and bright !

And not till her circle is low in the west
We'll cease from our dancing, or couch us to rest !

Lute, mute fall thy strings !
Hush, every voice that sings !
Low, slow, sleepy song,
Fade forest-aisles along !

Of all thy sweet music a love-song is best ! —
Thou hushest — we're silent — we sink into rest.

Richard Doyle (1824–1883)

ON New Year's Day, 1840, Richard Doyle took his father's advice and started to keep a diary, in laborious copperplate with copious illustrations. He had some misgivings about the project: 'First I thought I would, then I would not . . .' but finally he took the plunge. 'Hope I may be skinned alive if I don't go on with it.'

And go on with it he did, manfully, for eleven months and three days, for which persistence we can be very grateful. Without *Dick Doyle's Journal* we should not only lose a refreshing view of London life at the opening of Victoria's reign but also know much less about the young artist and his family background.

His father, John Doyle, was himself an artist, the celebrated 'HB', whose distinguished series of political sketches had substituted elegant portraiture for the savage caricaturing of Gillray or Cruikshank, and had set a new style of genial wit in cartoons. His own master had been a miniaturist and he took on the art training of his seven lively and talented sons and daughters, leaving the rest of their education to a tutor. The idea of the journal was to encourage Dick, who at fifteen had already decided on his profession, to be an accurate observer of the social scene.

There could not have been a better time to start. This was the young Queen's wedding year and Dick kept a watchful eye on the newspapers to see what excitement each day would offer in the way of processions, reviews of troops, illuminations, brass bands or Royal occasions. It was lucky for him that they lived close to Hyde Park so that when each day he and his younger brother walked out, in their neat belted tunics and peaked, tasselled caps, they were quickly in the midst of things. He seems to have developed a reporter's sixth sense for an impending scoop. ('Suppose we stop says I "Letts says Henry" and we did'.) A few 'anxious ladies and gentlemen' outside a confectioner's in Bond Street alert him to the fact that the Queen's wedding-cake is on view ('the great beast of a plum-cake some ten feet in circumference'); a solitary officer of the Blues in his state dress, riding slowly through the park, is doggedly followed by the brothers and he leads them to a magnificent, full-scale military review, attended by the Duke of Wellington and Prince Albert. They burrow their way through the heaving, good-humored crowd to get a close view of the wedding procession ('the Queen with a large viel over her head, looked actually beautiful'). Sometimes he sketches on the spot, sometimes from memory, but the sense of immediacy is never lost. To be lawfully let loose, a young artist, in London at this time, not shut away like most of his social equals in a public school, was surely a perfect method of learning through delight, which must have appealed to the elder Doyle's Horatian urbanity.

The system obviously worked well, for the sketches show a precocious professionalism which is at odds with the text. So much of the mature Richard Doyle is here already – the ingeniously intricate initial letters, the playful mediaevalism, the masterly composition, whether of bustling crowds or gracefully serried troops, the Lilliputian grotesques – that we need to turn to the mis-spellings, the schoolboyish pedantry and disarming outbursts to reassure ourselves that this actually is the work of the beaming shock-headed youth whose likeness is on every page. The household is obviously a happy one, with plenty of outings to the Zoo, the opera, the theatre, the Tower, all faithfully recorded but the event of the week is 'the show' which takes place each Sunday morning after chapel when all the young Doyles present their weekly artistic offerings, large or small, for their father's judgement. One sketch is of Dick, gazing apprehensively at his father, four brothers and two sisters over his unusually huge painting of Quentin Durward, 'four feet some inches by two feet some more inches'; another (more in tune with the talents shown in this volume) of him lying in bed, unable to sleep for the 'ideas' which assail him in the tiny flying shapes of elves, fairies, magicians, top-hatted, beaky bird which land on his counterpane to join the throng of aggressive little figures, tugging at his pillow and clambering up the sheets. If his eagerness 'to please Papa' strikes a later generation as somewhat obsessive it should be remembered that his mother was dead and that contemporaries would not have found his devoted dependence unnatural. Art was very much the shared element of the family and it is 'the most glorious day of the year' when they race up the steps of the National Gallery to visit the 1840 Academy exhibition, where Maclise and Landseer meet with Dick's heartfelt approval, but not 'the rather peculiar picture by W. Etty of Ten Virgins running about in front of a door (which is beautifully painted)'.

It is as a fellow-artist that he makes this judicious appraisal of Etty's achievement, for Richard Doyle had just begun to be known outside the domestic circle. The *Journal* is full of excited references to the printing of *The Eglinton Tournament*, his burlesque of that famous rain-soaked revival which his father had attended the previous year. With many a 'hurra' and 'crikey' Dick hails the arrival of the 'fifty hot pressed copies of the Tournament' which were brought up at a gratifying rate. His fascination with the Middle Ages (which he shared with so many Victorians) and his sense of the ridiculous had been put to good use and the comic little knights, jousting or wielding outsize swords, reappear constantly throughout the next decade in the corners of *Punch*. For in 1843 he got an introduction to the editor of that journal and found himself at the age of nineteen, a regular salaried contributor to it, along with such convivial colleagues as Leech, Thackeray and Jerrold.

Punch which had begun life as a mere 'Guffawgraph' only two years earlier was just beginning to take over its important role in English middle-class life. The large-scale political cartoons which were such an important feature of the weekly, were much more suited to Leech's powerful talents than Doyle's – though he improved with the years as a memorable picture of a skittles game testifies – with Mr Punch gleefully bowling over skittles which have got recognisable politicians' heads. But, on the whole, what the new recruit was used for was decorative work. Soon every issue was lightened with his playful headings and borders; his fantastically ingenious and ornate capitals; the large title letters which strode over the pages, sprouting hands and feet as they went or burgeoning with blossoms or holly; his minute, meticulously drawn illustrations – and always, somewhere, peering round a solid block of print or clambering between the lines, another fairy or comic dwarf or jester with cap and bells. After a time his insignia, the dicky-bird above or beside his initials, became very familiar to the readers of *Punch* and in 1849 he scored his major triumph.

Punch had had several covers since it started but it was

Doyle's design, an improved version of his 1844 cover, which lasted for over a century. It captured the spirit of the journal – its gaiety, irreverence (the British lion smiles complacently from the easel as Mr Punch raises his quill purposefully) and its never-ending stream of grotesquely comic ideas flowing from its cornucopia, which might have come straight from Doyle's own *Journal* or the folio of drawings, *Dick Kitcat's Book of Nonsense*.

In the same year he started a series of outline drawings to accompany the text of *Mr Pip's Diary* (written by Percival Leigh) which were enormously successful. The captions to the drawings were in archaic spelling – *Regente Strete of 4 of ye Clocke*, for instance – but there the connection with earlier centuries ended: the scenes were strictly contemporary and familiar to all *Punch* readers. In a letter Thackeray remarks on the fact that these gently satiric views of English society have proved a selling point and Holman Hunt claims that it was the *Banners and Customs of the English in 1849* which the pre-Raphaelites bought to study the grouping and which made his name 'a proverb throughout England'. The praise may seem excessive for these deft sketches of ladies and gentlemen wildly polka-ing or suffering a Lyttle Musyck in the drawing-room; of shoppers fingering swathes of silk in a fashionable haberdashers; of M.P.'s somnolently lolling through an Irish debate; of a sea of top-hats about to engulf Jenny Lind outside the Haymarket; of platters of whitebait, piled high in front of portly diners at Blackwall. But there was no doubt that Doyle had held up a mirror to the middle classes which enormously tickled their fancy and did not too greatly affront their vanity.

It was at this point, in 1850, at the time of the 'Papal aggression' scare, that *Punch* ran a series of virulent anti-papal cartoons which led Doyle, after unavailing protests, to resign from the paper. Years before his father had left Ireland because of religious persecution, and now his son, as staunch a Catholic, was to quit what he called 'the republic of Punch', a country till then congenial to him, which had given him security and full scope for his talents.

And so, at the age of twenty-seven, Doyle found himself in the strange situation, for the first time in his life, of not having to meet a weekly dead-line. He does not seem to have relished the freedom for Thackeray comments in 1853, 'Doyle is sad and has nothing to do' and asks him to illustrate *The Newcomes* 'to serve himself and his friend too'. It was a good move, for the illustrations are among the best that Doyle ever did. *The Newcomes* is a tamer book than *Vanity Fair* and Doyle's light witty touch and his excellence in facial expression suited it perfectly. He shared Thackeray's social background and could easily convey his nuances of snobbery and class-distinction. From then on he did a great deal of illustration – for Ruskin, Hughes and Oliphant, among others – although *In Fairyland* (1870) was a *tour de force* in colour which stands by itself. What he did not illustrate was *Alice in Wonderland*. Lewis Carroll met him at a party and asked him to take on the job but Doyle pleaded pressure of work: a Doyle *Alice*, instead of a Tenniel one, is an interesting thought.

After *The Newcomes* he still, however, had two very successful series up his sleeve. In the first of these, *The Foreign Tour of Brown, Jones and Robinson* (1855) he took up again a sort of comic strip he had begun earlier in *Punch*, an ongoing account of the exploits of three young men. Now he differentiated the trio much more sharply: Jones is very tall, with plaid trousers and his hat over his eyes; Robinson is tubby, self-indulgent and insular; Brown is small, the Doyle figure, with a mop of hair, an innocent look and a sketch pad always at the ready. These three innocents are savaged by Customs officials, enveloped in fog on a steam boat on the Rhine, moralise among the ruins at Heidelberg, get arrested in both Baden and Verona, are eaten alive by mosquitoes in Venice and lose their luggage in Dusseldorf; the very familiarity of the holiday misadventures surely constituted part of the appeal. Victorians of all ages took the travellers to their hearts, as Matthew Arnold's reference to his nine year old son, Tom, makes clear: 'I hear the little voice now in the next room talking to his mama about "Brown Jones and Robinson".'

Doyle's *Bird's Eye View of Society* was a series for the *Cornhill* (1861–63) of pull-out sketches which bring home better than any novels just what fashionable Victorians meant by 'a crush' at balls, afternoon parties, even at Science and Art Conversaziones. Under the title, *Small and Early: Refreshments*, surging billows of guests, plates held high, push and heave their way towards the loaded buffet tables; and in *Rotten Row in the Season* there is scarcely room to move for the bloods, leaning against the rails, their long legs stretched out at an incomparable Doyle angle – an obtuse angle, in both senses.

Throughout the '50s and '60s Doyle was a celebrity who had total entrée to the fashionable society which he had watched so vigilantly in his boyhood – and indeed continued to observe concealing his chuckles behind his hat. Like Thackeray he dined out a great deal – and like Thackeray also, he was in love with a married woman – Blanche, Lady Airlie – which may account for his being a bachelor all his life. His name figures so often in guest lists of memoirs, letters and diaries of the period that one is tempted to believe that he simply moved on from one dinner party to the next and one house-party to another. He stayed with Tennyson at Faringford; he was an habitué of Little Holland House (G. F. Watts); apart from Monckton Milnes he was the only non-political guest at Lady Palmerston's exclusive soirées at Cambridge House. Whoever talks about him, whether Thackeray, Charles Brookfield, Holman Hunt or George Eliot the effect is remarkably similar: 'Dear old Dicky Doyle'; 'Poor, dear Dicky Doyle'; 'Gentle, observant Dicky Doyle'; 'Unique, delightful Dicky Doyle'; 'The dear man'. They all praise – sometimes with a wondering, sometimes patronising note – his gentleness, nobility, purity of heart, high principles and sweetness of disposition. Malice indeed seems to have been left out of his nature; the edge that makes for really great satire was certainly lacking. But all were agreed; there could be no better companion than Dicky Doyle. Only William Rossetti strikes a more sober note, saying that Doyle gave him the impression of a man who had had some serious disappointment early in life and now 'had no particular object except to spend the passing hour pleasantly and to make it pleasant for others'. Whatever the reason, there can be no doubt that Dicky Doyle succeeded in doing that.

Dr Patricia Thomson
Reader in English at the University of Sussex